TO:

FROM:

Published by Sourcebooks Wonderland, an imprint of Sourcebooks Kids
P.O. Box 4410, Naperville, Illinois 60567-4410
(630) 961-3900
sourcebookskids.com

Library of Congress Cataloging-in-Publication Data is on file with the publisher.

Source of Production: 1010 Printing Asia Limited, Kwun Tong, Hong Kong, China
Date of Production: August 2022
Run Number: 5027579

Printed and bound in China.
OGP 10 9 8 7 6 5 4

HIDE AND SEEK
CHICAGO

BY ERIN GUENDELSBERGER   PICTURES BY MATTIA CERATO

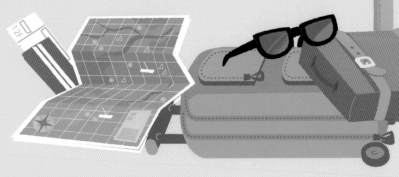

sourcebooks wonderland

WELCOME TO CHICAGO—THE BEST CITY IN THE WORLD!

I'm the mayor of this beautiful city, and I need your help. I'm creating an exhibit to feature the greatest parts of Chicago, and I am sending YOU on a quest to find the items that represent these places! This chart has everything you need to keep an eye out for and where you need to look.

PREPARE TO BE AMAZED—YOU'RE ABOUT TO EXPLORE AND LEARN ABOUT SOME OF THE BEST MUSEUMS, PARKS, AND ATTRACTIONS THE WORLD HAS EVER SEEN!

MAYOR

GRANT PARK

THE SHEDD AQUARIUM

O'HARE
INTERNATIONAL
AIRPORT

MUSEUM OF
SCIENCE + INDUSTRY

NORTH AVENUE
BEACH

THE ADLER PLANETARIUM

NAVY PIER

LINCOLN PARK
ZOO + CONSERVATORY

CHICAGO FRENCH MARKET

THE FIELD MUSEUM

THE ADLER PLANETARIUM

THE ADLER PLANETARIUM, the first in the Western Hemisphere, was funded by Chicago business leader **MAX ADLER** and opened to the public in 1930. Adler wanted to create an institution for popular astronomy education and dedicated the planetarium as a "classroom under the heavens." Total attendance at the Adler during the **CENTURY OF PROGRESS WORLD'S FAIR** (1933–1934) was more than 1.2 million people. Today, more than 500,000 people visit the Adler each year.

Guests to the Adler can experience sky shows, exhibits, and events. **THE DOANE OBSERVATORY** opened in 1977 as Chicago's first high-powered public telescope, making celestial objects trillions of miles away visible. **ATWOOD SPHERE,** Chicago's oldest planetarium, allows guests to experience the night sky over Chicago as it appeared in 1913, with a live guided tour to identify stars and the constellations they form.

CAN YOU FIND...

NOW THAT YOU'RE HERE, COULD YOU HELP ME FIND A FEW OTHER ITEMS?

CHICAGO FRENCH MARKET

This **EUROPEAN-STYLE MARKET** located in the West Loop neighborhood offers fresh ingredients and high-quality products from local vendors year-round. **THE FRENCH MARKET** opened its doors to Chicago in 2009 when the movement to support local farmers and incorporate a European-inspired marketplace spread across America. When at the market, visitors can pick up fresh food and flowers or grab a bite to eat from over thirty different vendors. Visitors can also enjoy concerts and other events held throughout the month.

CAN YOU FIND...

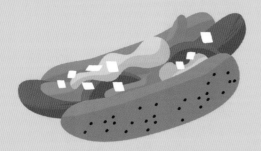

THE FIELD MUSEUM

After Chicago hosted the **WORLD'S COLUMBIAN EXPOSITION** in 1893, it was suggested that fair exhibits be purchased and used to create a museum. When initial fundraising efforts stalled, businessman and philanthropist **MARSHALL FIELD** donated $1 million, allowing plans for the museum to move forward. **THE FIELD MUSEUM**, initially called the Columbian Museum of Chicago, opened to the public on June 2, 1894. Its original location was in Jackson Park at what is now the Museum of Science and Industry. **THE FIELD MUSEUM** opened at its current home in Grant Park in 1921.

Visitors today can enjoy an array of exhibits, such as birds, gems, jades, meteorites, and many different animals. There are exhibits about the evolution of our planet, ancient Egypt, the Americas, Africa, the Pacific, and dinosaurs like Sue, the famous *Tyrannosaurus rex*.

CAN YOU FIND...

WOW, THERE'S A LOT HERE! CAN YOU HELP ME FIND THESE THINGS?

NAVY PIER

DANIEL BURNHAM, one of the world's most respected architects in the early 1900s, envisioned a public pier that would transform Chicago's lakefront into a place for people to visit and interact. **MUNICIPAL PIER NO. 2** opened to the public in 1916, and at 292 feet wide and 3,040 feet into Lake Michigan, it is the longest public pier in the world. In 1927, the pier was renamed **NAVY PIER** as a tribute to WWI Navy personnel.

NAVY PIER has been used for military training grounds, an extension of the University of Illinois, trade shows, and large public events. The pier was renovated and reopened in 1995, featuring a mix of shops, restaurants, attractions, and a Ferris wheel. In 2016, the new **CENTENNIAL WHEEL** replaced the original wheel and is the fifth tallest in the country!

CAN YOU FIND...

CAN YOU ALSO LOOK FOR THESE THINGS?

GRANT PARK

Known as "CHICAGO'S FRONT YARD," Grant Park dates back to 1835, when Chicago citizens lobbied to protect the lakefront from commercial development. It was officially named LAKE PARK in 1847. In 1901, the park's name was changed to GRANT PARK to honor U.S. President ULYSSES S. GRANT.

Today, this 319-acre park includes the Art Institute of Chicago, the Field Museum of Natural History, Shedd Aquarium, Adler Planetarium, Millennium Park, and Maggie Daley Park. The CLARENCE BUCKINGHAM MEMORIAL FOUNTAIN, one of the world's largest fountains, was dedicated in 1927 and is the centerpiece of Grant Park. Grant Park is home to a wide array of music, food, and cultural festivals throughout the year. It's also the site of the start and finish lines for the CHICAGO MARATHON!

CAN YOU FIND...

NOW THAT YOU'RE HERE, WOULD YOU MIND HELPING ME FIND A FEW OTHER ITEMS?

x2

THE SHEDD AQUARIUM

THE SHEDD AQUARIUM was a gift to Chicago from **JOHN G. SHEDD,** who began as a stock boy and later became president of the Marshall Field & Company department store. Shedd wanted to create an aquarium to rival those in Europe, and it opened on May 30, 1930. It was the **FIRST INLAND AQUARIUM** in the world with permanent saltwater exhibits as well as freshwater habitats and took a million gallons of ocean water from Key West, Florida to fill the exhibits.

Nearly two million guests visit the aquarium every year to see over **32,000 ANIMALS** from the Amazon, Caribbean, Great Lakes, oceans, and beyond. Live animal presentations demonstrate how animals like dolphins, sea lions, and beluga whales are trained and cared for. Visitors who want a hands-on experience can touch stingrays, sea stars, and sturgeons.

CAN YOU FIND...

$8.99

MUSEUM OF SCIENCE + INDUSTRY

THE MUSEUM OF SCIENCE AND INDUSTRY was founded by Julius Rosenwald and opened in 1933 in a building originally constructed for the **1893 WORLD'S COLUMBIAN EXPOSITION.** Today, it is the largest science museum in the Western Hemisphere and one of the largest in the world, hosting about **1.5 MILLION GUESTS** each year!

The museum offers numerous hands-on exhibits and more than **35,000 ARTIFACTS.** Visitors can explore the museum's original interactive experience, the coal mine, and discover the science behind submarines, storms, farms, and all forms of transportation. There is a mirror maze, a chick hatchery, a massive model railroad display, one of America's first diesel-electric streamlined passenger trains, and the **WORLD'S LARGEST PINBALL MACHINE!** In addition to a domed theater and a large auditorium, the museum also has **TWELVE LEARNING LABS.**

CAN YOU FIND...

WHILE YOU'RE HERE, CAN YOU ALSO FIND THESE OBJECTS?

NORTH AVENUE BEACH

NORTH AVENUE BEACH, one of Chicago's most popular beaches, is located in Lincoln Park beside LAKE MICHIGAN. The creation of the beach was funded through the WORKS PROGRESS ADMINISTRATION (WPA), part of President Franklin D. Roosevelt's "NEW DEAL." Construction began in 1939. The beach and an accompanying beach house—designed to look like a ship—were dedicated in July of 1940. The beach house eventually deteriorated, and a new beach house of similar design was built in 1999.

Visitors to the beach today can enjoy water, sand, and the BEACH HOUSE. There are also restaurants, stores, and rental activities—bikes, kayaks, Jet Skis, paddleboards, wakeboards, and more. An open-air sports facility offers roller hockey, dodgeball, fitness classes, and special events.

CAN YOU FIND...

O'HARE INTERNATIONAL AIRPORT

In 1945, **ORCHARD FIELD**, an aircraft assembly plant, was selected as the site for a new Chicago airport. Chicago City Council renamed it to honor naval aviator **LT. CMDR. EDWARD H. "BUTCH" O'HARE**, a Medal of Honor recipient from Chicago who died in WWII. The airport opened to commercial air traffic in 1955. O'Hare became the **"WORLD'S BUSIEST AIRPORT"** in 1962, serving 10 million passengers, which has only increased through the years—with 30 million by 1968, 50 million by 1986, and more than 70 million by 1997.

Today, the airport has 191 gates and eight active runways. Visitors can enjoy a variety of shops and restaurants. The airport exhibits art from local artists and also has a unique **URBAN GARDEN**, the first aeroponic garden at any airport in the world!

CAN YOU FIND...

DUTY FREE

DUTY

EXIT

× DEPARTURES

TIME	DESTINATION	FLIGHT #	GATE
10:15	BERLIN	A7889	12
10:25	PORTLAND	B3612	34
11:00	ROME	Z9000	04
11:05	CALGARY	D2145	10
11:45	MEXICO CITY	J8998	03
12:00	MIAMI	A2098	09
12:25	SYDNEY	B4567	45

BLUE BIRD COMPANY

Mr. Lee

NOW THAT YOU'RE HERE, COULD YOU HELP ME FIND A FEW OTHER ITEMS?

LINCOLN PARK ZOO + CONSERVATORY

LINCOLN PARK ZOO was founded in 1868 when the park commissioners were gifted a pair of swans by commissioners from NEW YORK'S CENTRAL PARK. Next came a ten dollar bear and an orphaned gorilla! The SEAL POOL, originally constructed in 1879, is one of the oldest and most popular zoo exhibits. The LION HOUSE, built in 1912, is a historic landmark right at the heart of the zoo. A 29,000-foot, indoor/outdoor exhibit hosting chimpanzees and gorillas is the most expensive building ever constructed at a zoo.

There are still swans, seals, lions, bears, and gorillas living in the FORTY-NINE ACRE ZOO today, part of more than 200 SPECIES and 1100 ANIMALS, not counting fish and insects. Visitors can see animals from tigers, to crocodiles, to penguins, and many more!

CAN YOU FIND...